World War II Posters

By Philip Martin McCaulay

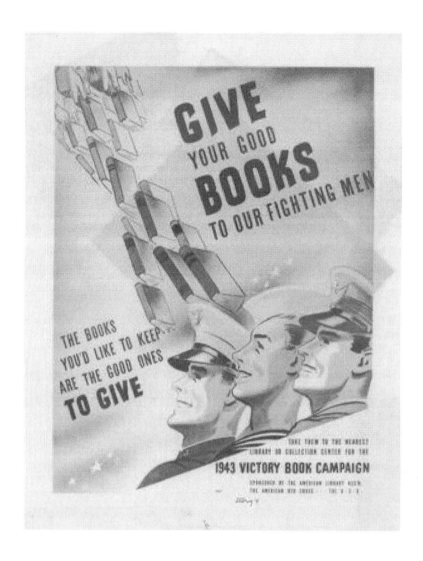

World War II Posters

Preface

In 1942, after the United States entered World War II following the attack on Pearl Harbor in December 1941, the federal government started producing and distributing informational materials to attract and encourage public support for the money, material resources, labor, and personal sacrifices needed to mount a successful war effort.

Large federal agencies such as the Department of War, the Treasury Department and the Department of Agriculture distributed their own informational materials. To consolidate the distribution of war-related pamphlets, handbooks, and posters, a new agency was created. On June 13, 1942, President Franklin Roosevelt signed Executive Order 9182, which created the Office of War Information (OWI).

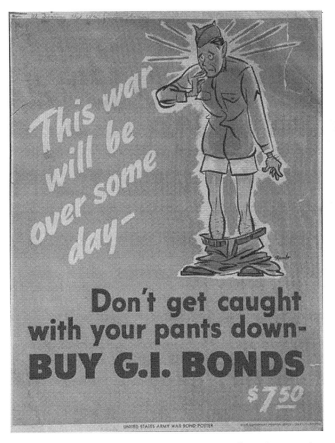

One of the functions of the OWI was the distribution of posters. The OWI distributed posters on a national scale to post offices, schools, and railroad stations. They also depended on local civic groups to distribute posters. Defense Councils in each community were instructed to form a committee to regularly receive posters. The committee determined the number needed by the community, selected posting locations, and set up a route and distribution system. New posters were distributed at the beginning of each month and were put up as soon as possible.

Table of Contents

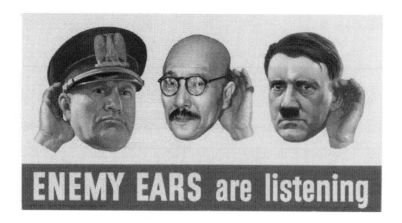

Savings and Investment

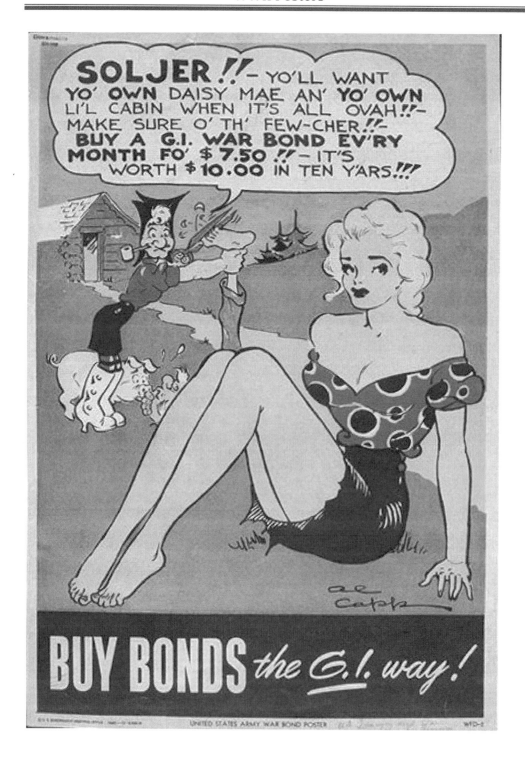

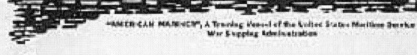

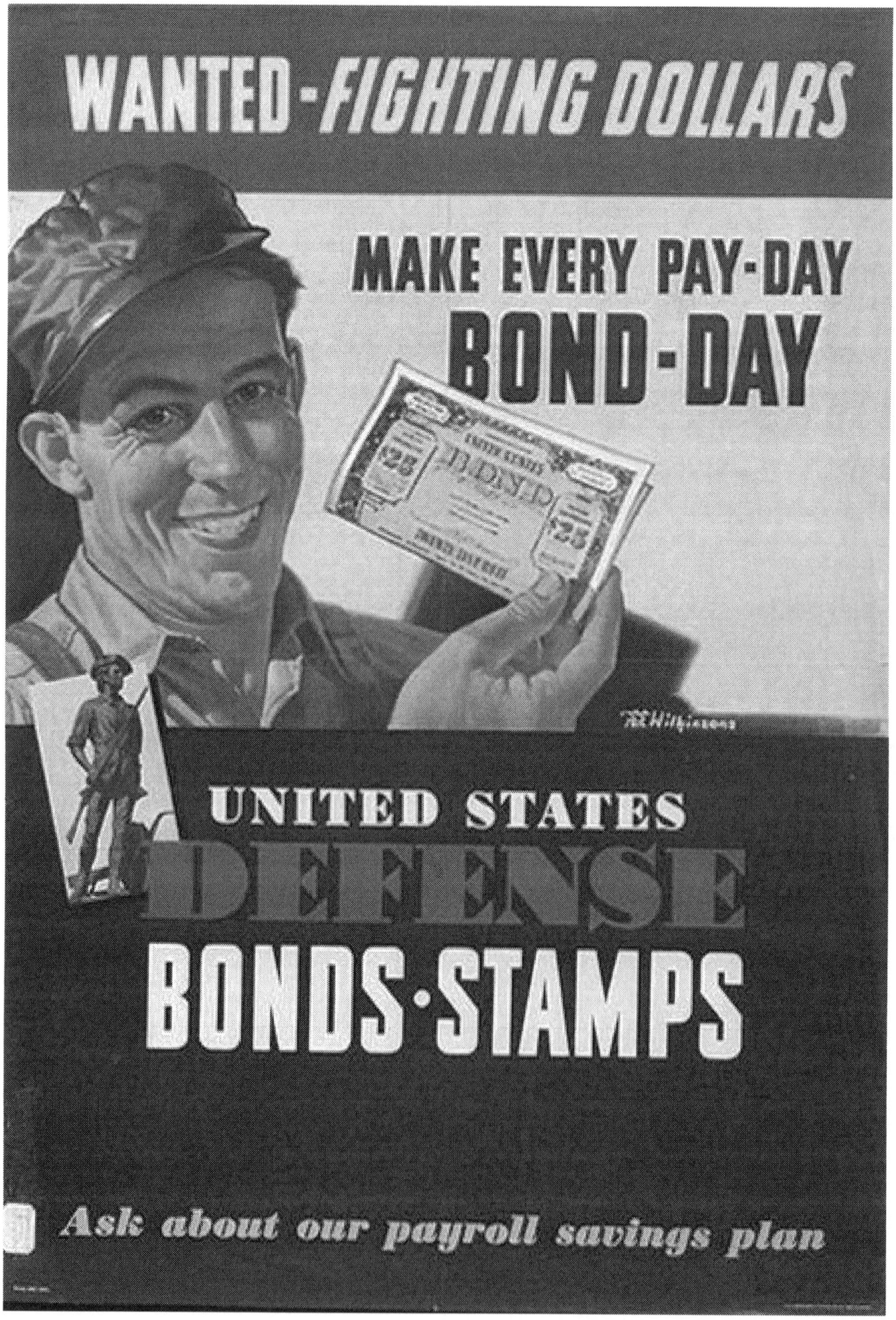
WANTED-FIGHTING DOLLARS
MAKE EVERY PAY-DAY
BOND-DAY
UNITED STATES
DEFENSE
BONDS·STAMPS
Ask about our payroll savings plan

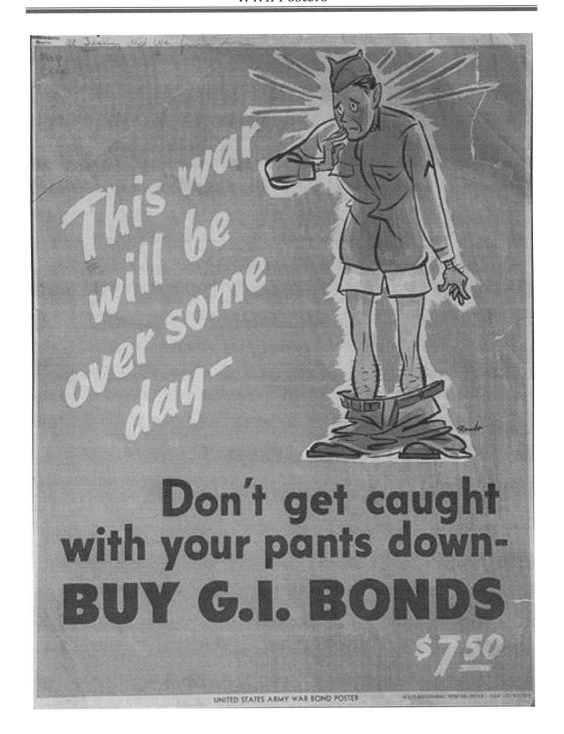

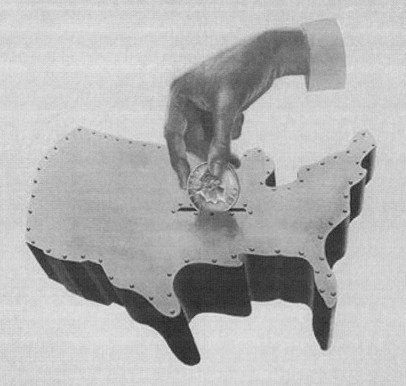

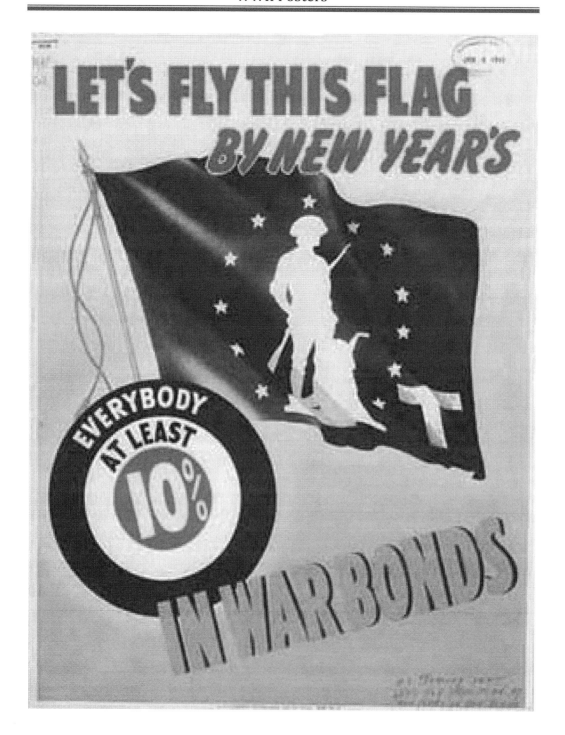

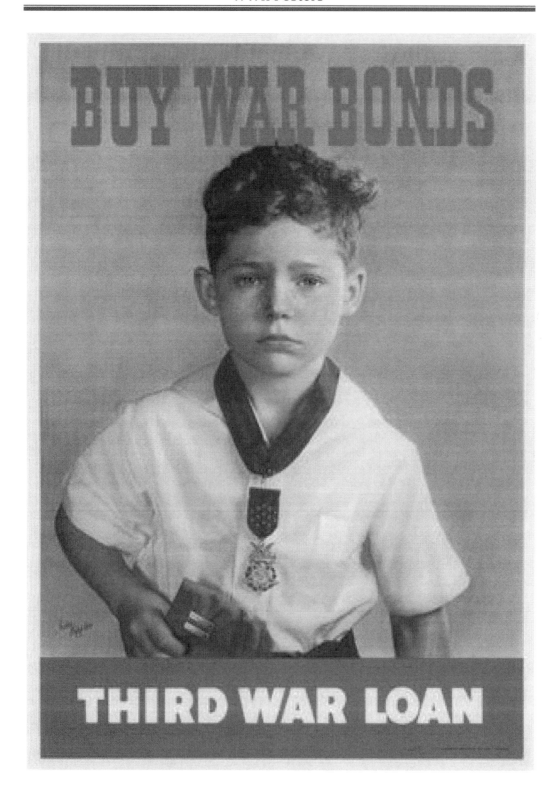

Productivity and Innovation

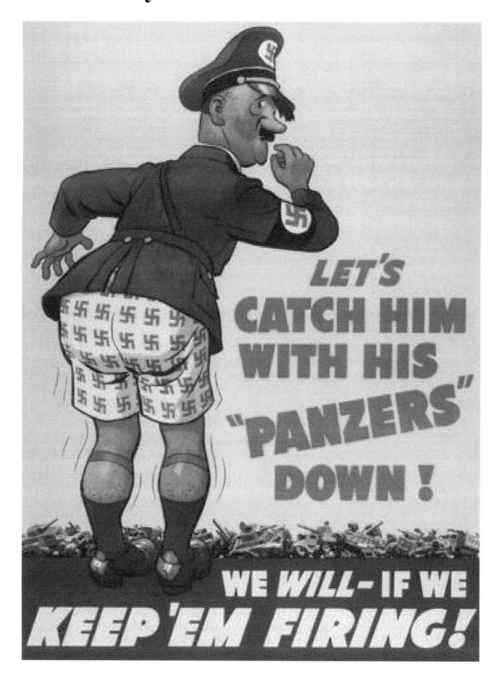

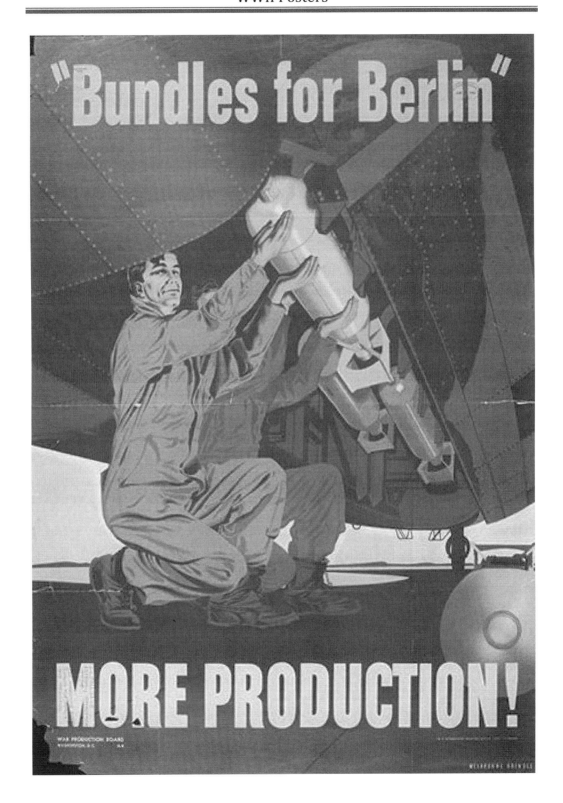

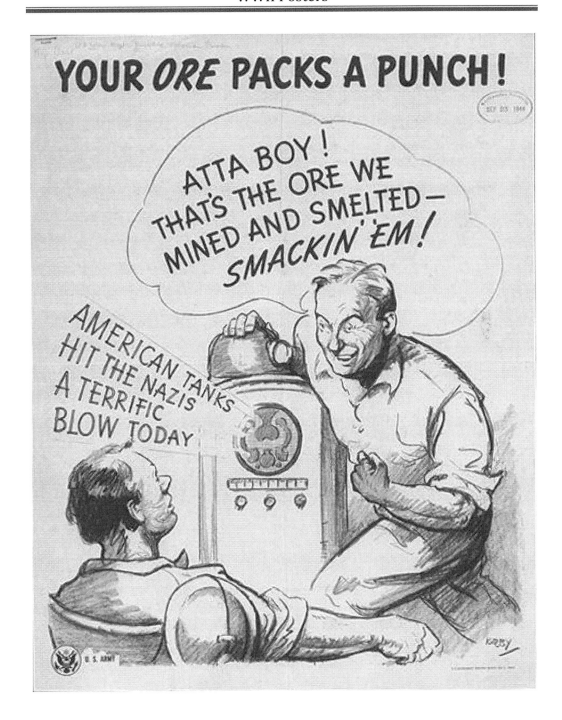

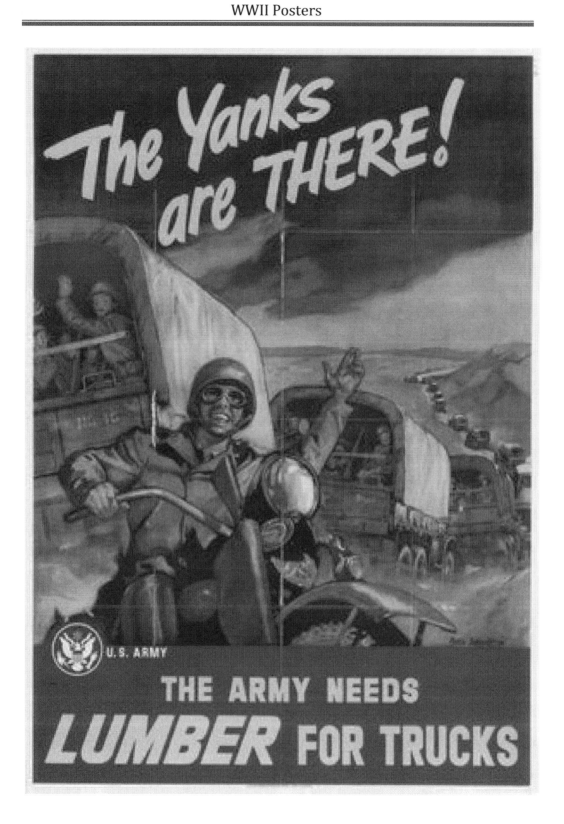

"Every job is a fighting man's job. Minutes count with freedom at stake. Let's cram them full of work!"

PRODUCE FOR VICTORY!

"You make 'em, buddy . . . we'll use 'em . . . and how! We're all soldiers together. Our victories in battle come right after your victories in production."

PRODUCE FOR VICTORY!

"Man for man, America's workers
and America's soldiers are the best in
the world! We helped them build our
nation . . . we'll help them defend it."

PRODUCE FOR VICTORY!

"Gosh! Look at 'em fly! My Pop helps make those planes. With flyers like that and workers like my Pop...us Americans are sure gonna win this scrap!"

PRODUCE FOR VICTORY!

WOMEN'S BUREAU

ARMS AND THE WOMEN HELP WITH DEFENSE

ARTILLERY AMMUNITION—WOMEN ARE DOING MANY JOBS HERE

GAGING AND WEIGHING CARTRIDGES IN AN ENDLESS ROW

A COMFORTABLE JOB—INSPECTING SMALL-ARMS CARTRIDGES

KEEP 'EM SMILING—THE WORK GOES BETTER

ASSEMBLING GAS MASKS

ACCURACY IS HER WATCHWORD

ASSEMBLING WIRE HARNESS FOR ARMY TRUCKS

SPRAYING THE GARDEN? GUESS AGAIN, IT'S AN AUTOMOTIVE PROCESS

SHE HELPS TO MAKE THE WHEELS OF WAR GO 'ROUND

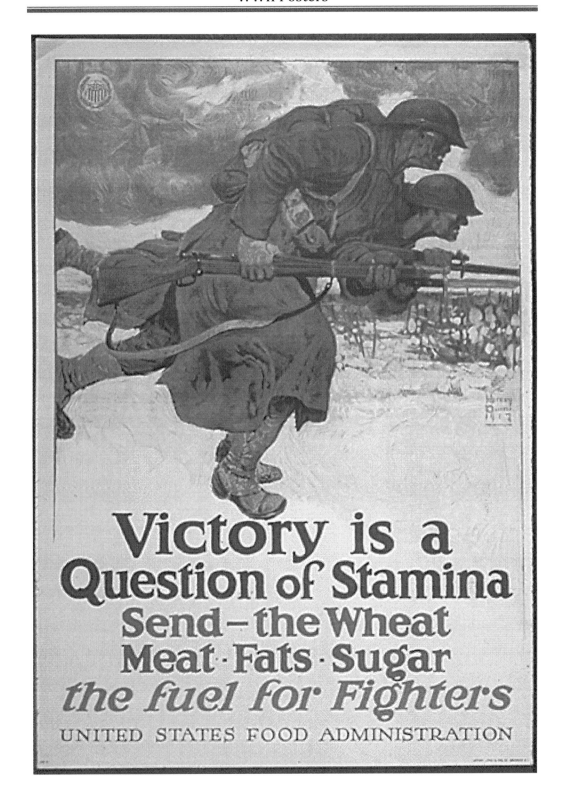

Service and Support

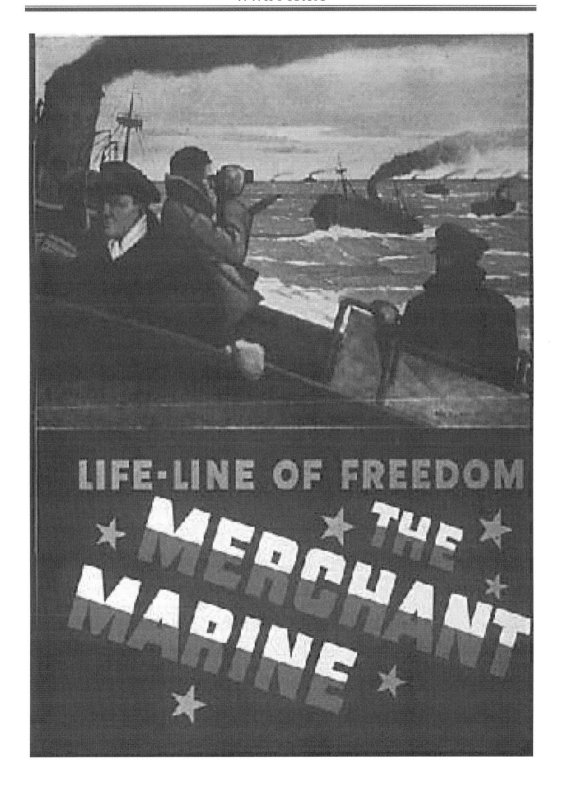

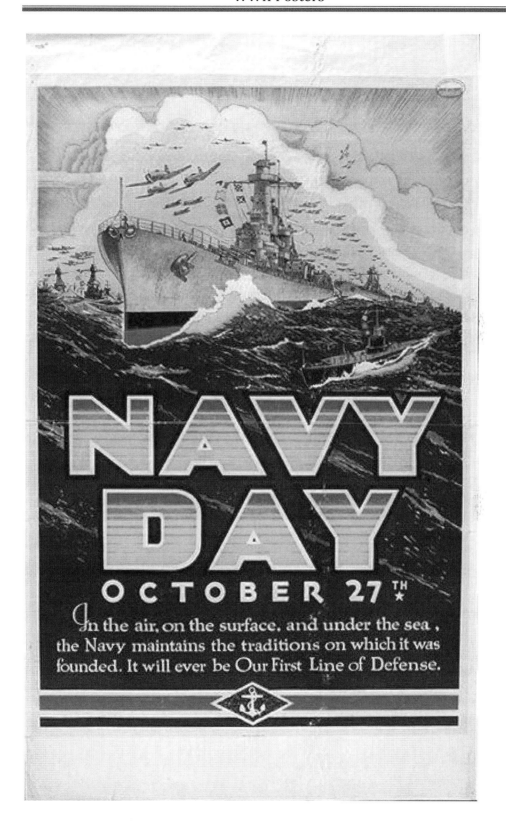

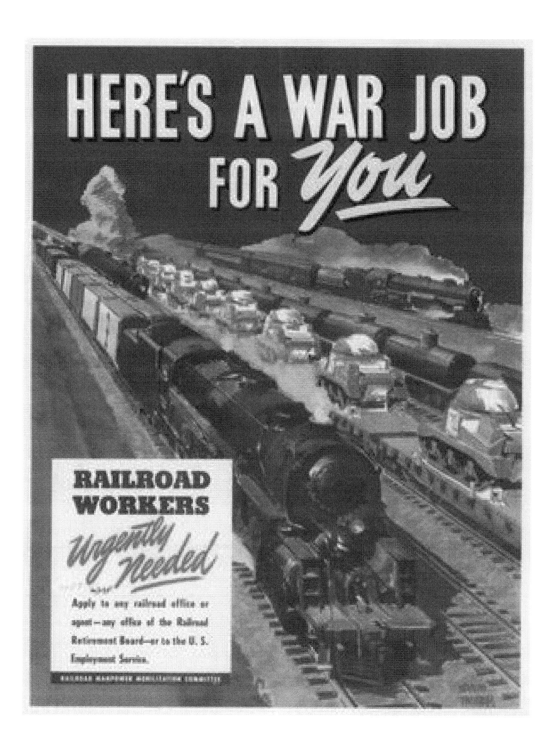

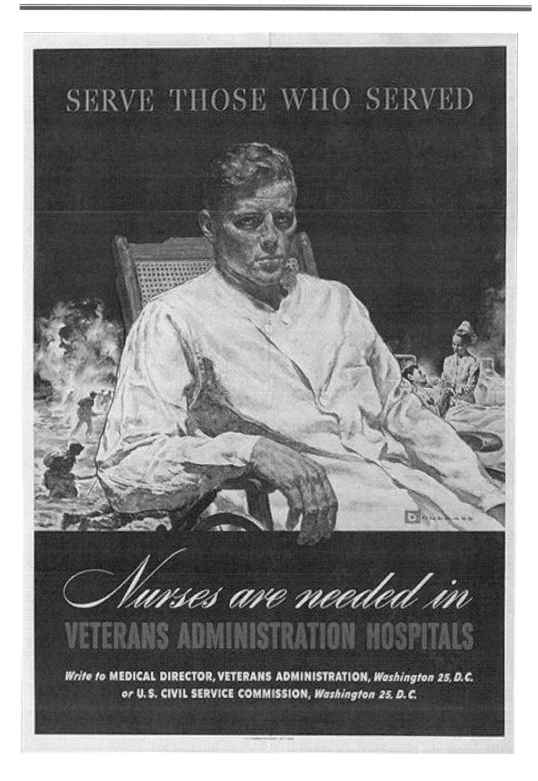

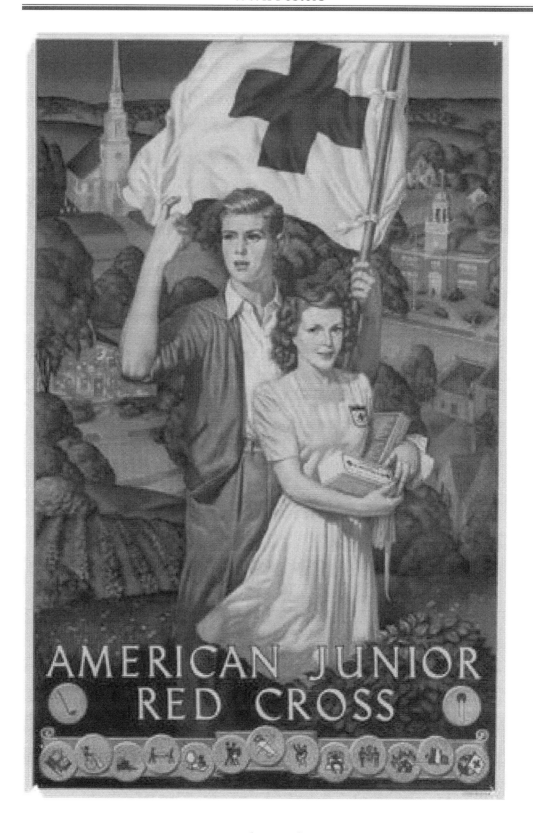

Environmentalism and Conservation

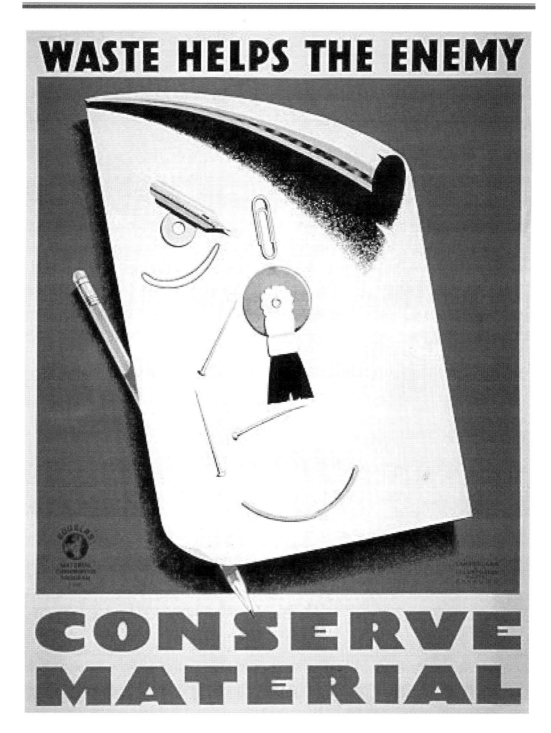

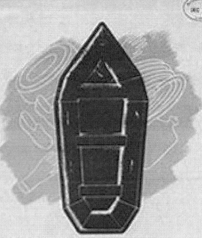

A Gas Mask requires 1.11 pounds of rubber

A Life Raft requires 17 to 100 pounds of rubber

A Scout Car requires 306 pounds of rubber

A Heavy Bomber requires 1,825 pounds of rubber

America needs your SCRAP RUBBER

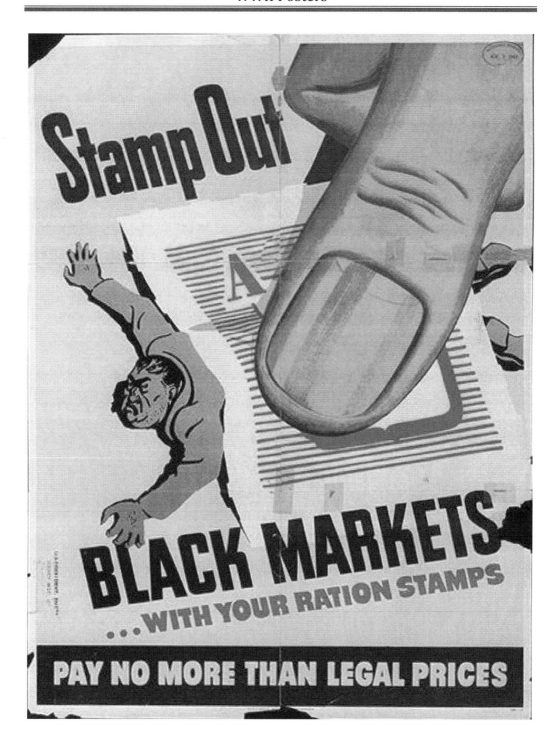

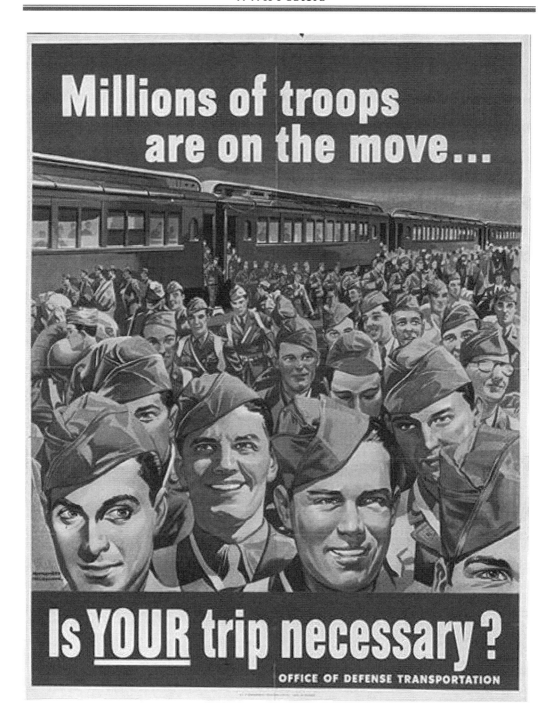

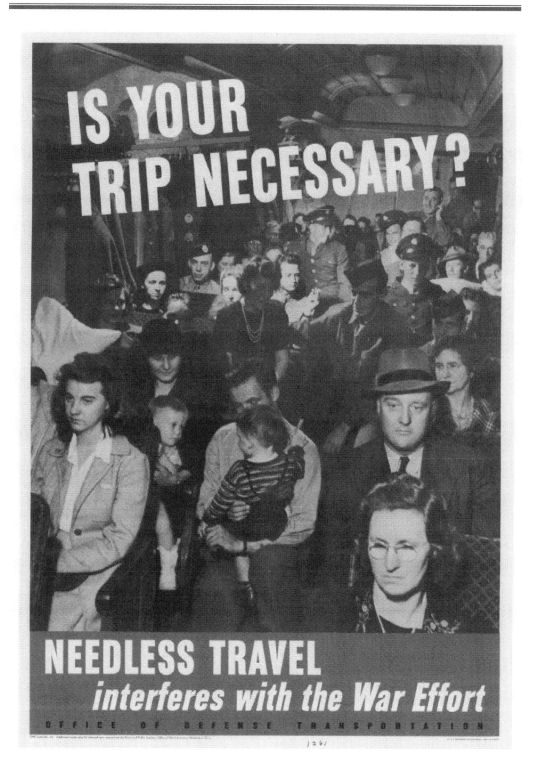

Here's a war job all America may be proud of. The rise in the wartime cost of living today is less than half the World War I increase... only the patriotic cooperation of the public and businessmen with the government's price control program made this record possible... let's keep up the good work by keeping the **Home Front Pledge:**

"I pay no more than ceiling prices.. ..I pay my ration points in full."

UNITED STATES OFFICE OF PRICE ADMINISTRATION

Security and Trust

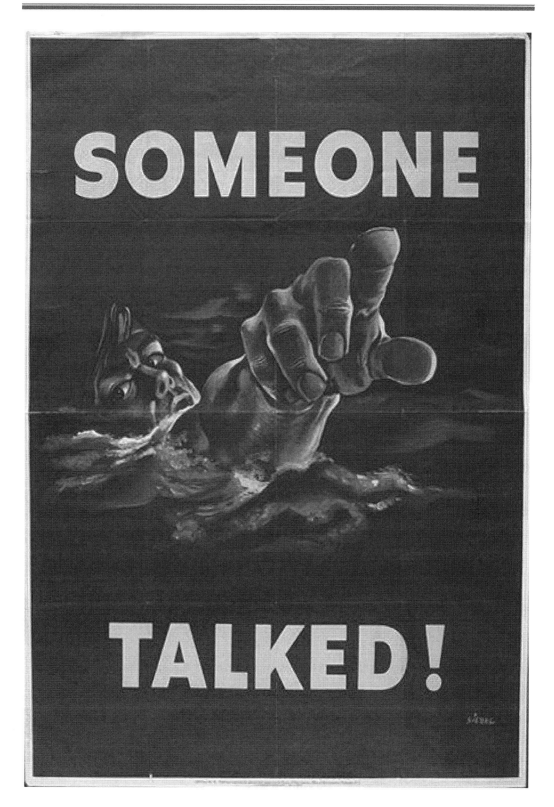

Freedom and Sacrifice

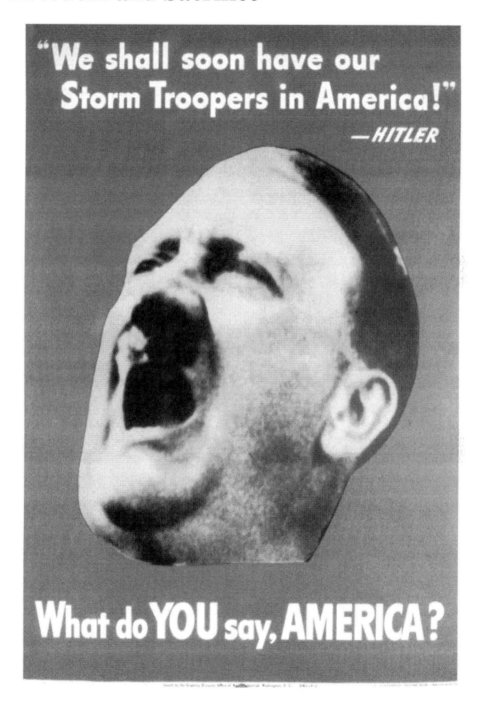

"I am looking forward to dictating peace to the United States in the White House at Washington"
—ADMIRAL YAMAMOTO
What do YOU say, AMERICA?

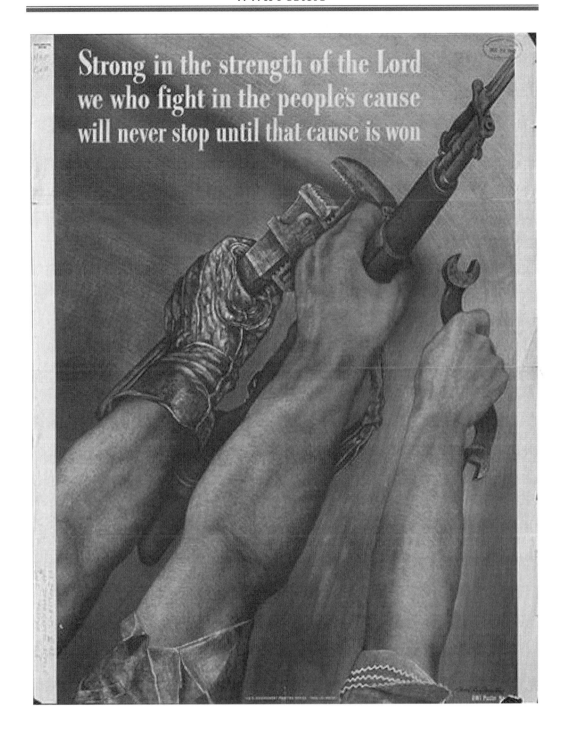

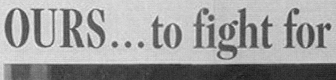

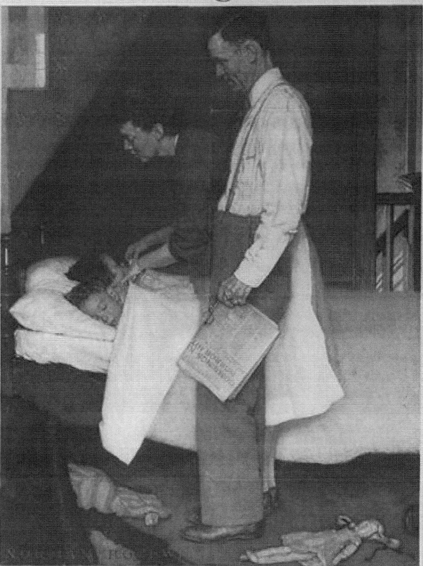

Ten years ago:
THE NAZIS BURNED
THESE BOOKS

...*but free Americans*
CAN STILL READ THEM

Friends and Allies

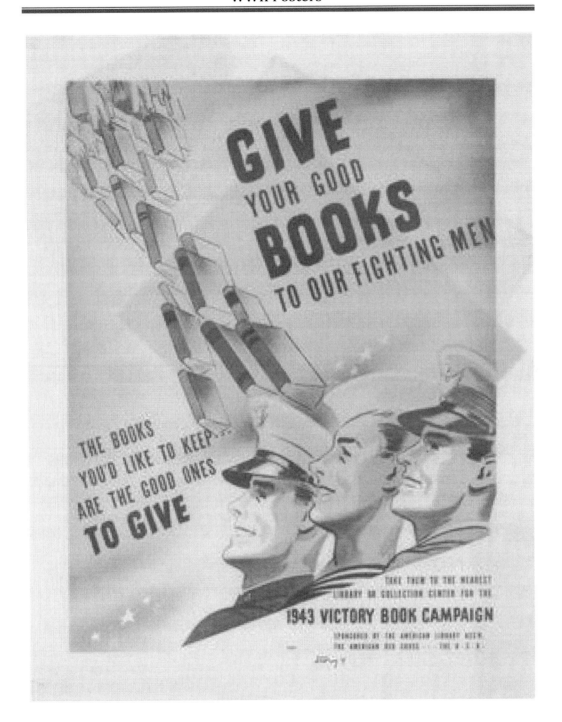

Health and Safety

U.S. NEEDS US STRONG
EAT NUTRITIONAL FOOD
DO YOUR PART IN THE NATIONAL NUTRITION PROGRAM
Office of Defense Health and Welfare Services, Washington, D. C.

EAT THE RIGHT FOOD

America needs you strong

Follow the rules of good nutrition—eat these foods every day:

MILK—at least a pint for everyone, more for children —or cheese, or evaporated or dried milk.

ORANGES, TOMATOES, GRAPEFRUIT, OR RAW CABBAGE—at least one of these.

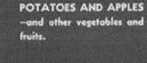

VEGETABLES—GREEN, LEAFY, AND YELLOW— one big helping or more— some raw, some cooked.

POTATOES AND APPLES —and other vegetables and fruits.

LEAN MEAT, POULTRY, OR FISH—or sometimes dried beans or peas.

EGGS—at least 3 or 4 a week, cooked any way you choose or in "made" dishes.

BREAD AND CEREAL— whole grain products or enriched bread and flour.

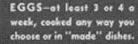

FATS, SWEETS, and seasonings as you like them.

DO YOUR PART in the National Nutrition Program · Work With Your Local Nutrition Committee

Office of Defense Health and Welfare Services, Washington, D. C.

Victory Gardens

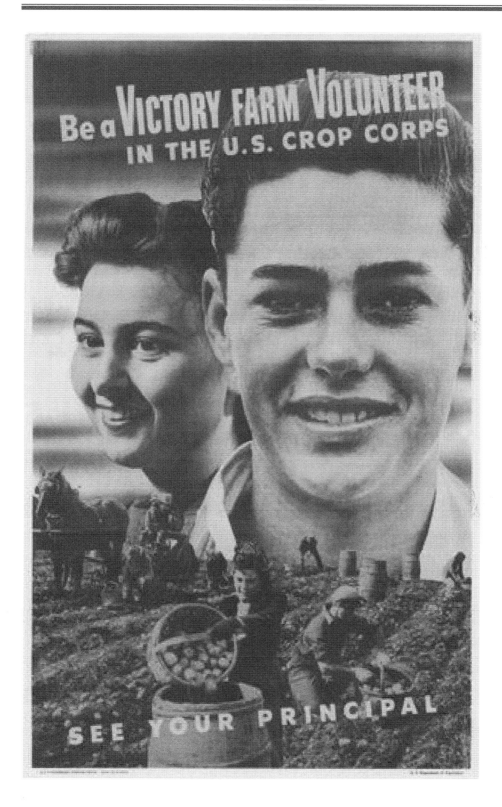

Reference List

Denison University, available at http://www.denison.edu/

George C. Marshall Foundation, available at http://library.marshallfoundation.org/

Google Images, available at http://images.google.com/

National Archives, available at http://www.archives.gov/

National Museum of American History, available at http://americanhistory.si.edu/

Norman Rockwell Museum, available at http://www.nrm.org/

Northwestern University, available at http://www.library.northwestern.edu/

Rutgers University, available at http://www.libraries.rutgers.edu/

West Texas A & M University, available at http://www.wtamu.edu/library/

University of North Texas, available at http://digital.library.unt.edu/

Wikipedia, available at http://en.wikipedia.org/wiki/

About the Author

Philip Martin McCaulay is an actuary with a degree in mathematics from Indiana University. He has sold thousands of non-fiction books in the fields of pensions, investments, finance, real estate, massage therapy, card games, cooking, and history. He volunteers to send books to soldiers through Operation Paperback.

Made in the USA
Charleston, SC
29 July 2013